THE COMPLETE GUIDE TO SWIMMING POOL CONSTRUCTION AND MAINTENANCE

Learn the Basics of Constructing Your Own Pool and Maintenance

Practices for Lasting Comfort and Relaxation

Elaine Weber

Disclaimer

The information provided in this book, "The Complete Guide to Swimming Pool Construction and Maintenance," is intended for general guidance and informational purposes only. The author and publisher are not liable for any errors, omissions, or damages arising from the use or misuse of the information presented. Readers are advised to consult professionals and local regulations for specific advice and guidelines pertaining to their individual swimming pool projects.

Table of Contents

TABLE OF CONTENTS 5

INTRODUCTION 8

CHAPTER 1: INTRODUCTION TO SWIMMING POOL
CONSTRUCTION 12

CHAPTER 2: PLANNING AND DESIGNING YOUR
SWIMMING POOL 17

CHAPTER 3: POOL CONSTRUCTION MATERIALS
AND EQUIPMENT 24

CHAPTER 4: EXCAVATION AND FOUNDATION
PREPARATION 30

CHAPTER 5: POOL PLUMBING AND ELECTRICAL
SYSTEMS 36

CHAPTER 6: INSTALLING POOL FILTERS, PUMPS,
AND HEATERS 43

CHAPTER 7: POOL DECKING AND SURROUNDING LANDSCAPING 49

CHAPTER 8: POOL FINISHES AND SURFACE TREATMENTS 55

CHAPTER 9: POOL SAFETY MEASURES AND REGULATIONS 60

CHAPTER 10: WATER TREATMENT AND CHEMICAL BALANCING 65

CHAPTER 11: POOL MAINTENANCE BASICS 71

CHAPTER 12: TROUBLESHOOTING COMMON POOL ISSUES 78

CHAPTER 13: POOL REPAIRS AND RENOVATIONS 85

CHAPTER 14: WINTERIZING AND SEASONAL POOL CARE 93

CONCLUSION 100

Introduction

Welcome to "The Complete Guide to Swimming Pool Construction and Maintenance"! Whether you're a homeowner considering building a new swimming pool or a pool maintenance professional looking to enhance your skills, this book is your ultimate resource.

Swimming pools are more than just places to cool off; they are a symbol of relaxation, entertainment, and luxury. However, constructing and maintaining a swimming pool requires careful planning, knowledge of various construction techniques, and an understanding of proper maintenance practices. This comprehensive guide aims to equip you with all the information you need to create and maintain your dream pool.

In the following chapters, we will explore every aspect of swimming pool construction and maintenance in great detail. We'll start with the fundamentals, discussing the importance of proper planning and design. You'll learn about different pool types, sizes, and shapes, as well as considerations for location, permits, and budgeting. We'll delve into the various materials and equipment used in pool construction, from excavation and foundation preparation to plumbing and electrical systems installation.

Once your pool is built, we'll guide you through the installation of essential components like filters, pumps, and heaters, ensuring optimal performance and energy efficiency. We'll also explore options for pool decking and landscaping, providing you with ideas to enhance the aesthetics and functionality of your pool area.

Ensuring the utmost safety of swimming pools is our top priority. Therefore, we will allocate a complete chapter to address safety precautions and pertinent regulations. You'll learn about fencing requirements, lifeguarding considerations, and pool covers to keep your pool secure and protect your loved ones.

Proper water treatment and chemical balancing are vital for maintaining a clean and healthy pool. We'll cover the basics of water chemistry, including pH levels, chlorine, and other sanitizers. You'll gain insights into testing and balancing water parameters, preventing common issues like algae growth and cloudy water.

To keep your pool in pristine condition, regular maintenance is essential. We'll provide step-by-step instructions for cleaning and vacuuming the pool, as well as guidance on routine tasks such as skimming debris and cleaning filters. Additionally, we'll address troubleshooting common pool problems, from leaks and equipment malfunctions to water chemistry imbalances.

Over time, you may consider making repairs or renovating your pool. We'll discuss the common issues that arise and guide you through the process of fixing them. From cracks in the pool structure to worn-out surfaces, you'll learn how to identify and address these problems effectively.

Lastly, we'll cover winterizing your pool and preparing it for the offseason. Proper seasonal care ensures that your pool remains in good condition and is ready for use when warmer weather returns.

By the end of this book, you'll be equipped with the knowledge and confidence to embark on your swimming pool construction or maintenance journey. So, let's dive in and discover the world of swimming pool excellence!

Chapter 1: Introduction to Swimming Pool Construction

Swimming pools have always been a source of joy and relaxation for people of all ages. Whether you envision a small backyard oasis or a grand resort-style pool, the construction process requires careful planning and a solid understanding of the various steps involved. In this chapter, we will lay the foundation for your swimming pool construction journey by introducing you to the key considerations and initial steps.

Understanding Your Pool Needs and Goals

Before embarking on any construction project, it is essential to determine your specific needs and goals for the pool. Consider the primary purpose of the pool—will it be primarily for recreation, exercise, or a combination of both? Do you envision a specific design or style that complements your property? By clarifying your objectives, you can make informed decisions throughout the construction process.

Assessing Your Property

The next step is to assess your property to determine the best location and size for your swimming pool. Factors such as available space, topography, existing structures, and utility lines will influence the pool's placement. It is crucial to work closely with a professional pool designer or architect who can assess the site and provide valuable insights.

Pool Design and Style

The design and style of your pool contribute significantly to its overall aesthetics and functionality. There are various pool types to choose from, including inground, above-ground, lap pools, and infinity pools. Consider factors such as the size and shape that best fit your property, as well as any additional features like waterfalls, spa areas, or diving boards that you desire.

Budgeting and Financial Considerations

Constructing a swimming pool involves financial investment, and setting a realistic budget is crucial. Consider not only the initial construction costs but also long-term maintenance expenses. It is advisable to obtain multiple quotes from reputable pool builders and factor in potential additional costs for landscaping, fencing, lighting, and water treatment systems.

Permits and Legal Requirements

Before proceeding with the construction of your swimming pool, it is important to familiarize yourself with local regulations and obtain the necessary permits. Depending on your location, there may be specific requirements regarding pool fencing, safety measures, setback distances, and water conservation. Compliance with these regulations is essential to ensure the safety and legality of your pool.

Choosing a Pool Contractor

Selecting a reliable and experienced pool contractor is paramount to the success of your project. Research potential contractors, check their credentials, and request references from previous clients. Evaluate their expertise, track record, and ability to understand and meet your specific needs. A skilled contractor will guide you through the entire construction process and ensure a smooth execution.

Project Timeline and Construction Phases

Understanding the timeline and construction phases will give you a clear picture of what to expect throughout the process. From initial site preparation and excavation to plumbing and electrical installations, each phase requires careful coordination and attention to detail.

Familiarize yourself with these stages to monitor progress and address any concerns that may arise.

Maintenance and Long-Term Care

Even before your pool is complete, it is crucial to consider its long-term maintenance requirements. Regular upkeep, such as cleaning, water treatment, and equipment inspections, will ensure that your pool remains clean, safe, and inviting for years to come. Familiarize yourself with recommended maintenance practices and consider investing in automation systems or professional pool maintenance services.

As you embark on your swimming pool construction journey, remember that proper planning and attention to detail are key. By understanding your needs, collaborating with professionals, and adhering to legal requirements, you will lay a solid foundation for a beautiful and enjoyable swimming pool. In the following chapters, we will delve into each aspect of the construction process in more detail, guiding you towards a successful pool project.

Chapter 2: Planning and Designing Your Swimming Pool

We will move now into the planning and design phase, where you will define your pool's purpose and features.

Begin by considering how you envision using your pool. Will it primarily be for recreation and entertainment, or do you have specific exercise or therapeutic goals in mind? Understanding the primary purpose of your pool will help determine its size, shape, and additional features.

Think about the features and amenities you would like to incorporate into your pool design. Would you like a shallow area for children to play, a spa or hot tub for relaxation, or perhaps a swim-up bar for entertaining guests? By identifying these desired features early on, you can work with your pool designer to create a comprehensive and functional design.

Pool Size and Shape

The size and shape of your pool will depend on several factors, including available space, budget, and intended use. Consider the dimensions of your property and how the pool will fit into the overall layout. Keep in mind that local regulations may have specific requirements for setbacks and distances from property lines or existing structures.

When determining the size of your pool, think about the number of people who will use it regularly and the activities they will engage in. If you plan to incorporate lap swimming or water exercises, you'll need sufficient length and depth. On the other hand, if your primary focus is on recreational activities, you may prioritize a larger shallow area or additional features like slides or waterfalls.

The shape of your pool can contribute to its overall aesthetics and functionality. Rectangular pools are classic and versatile, while freeform or kidney-shaped pools offer a more organic and natural look. Consider your personal preferences, architectural style, and landscaping when deciding on the pool's shape.

Pool Placement and Orientation

The placement and orientation of your pool are crucial considerations for maximizing its usability and optimizing sunlight exposure. Take into account factors such as privacy, existing landscaping, and the natural topography of your property.

Consider the position of the sun throughout the day and how it will affect the pool's temperature and lighting. Most people prefer their pools to receive ample sunlight, but you may also want to incorporate shaded areas for relief from the sun during hot summer days. Additionally, consider the views from various vantage points, both within and outside your home, to ensure an aesthetically pleasing pool layout.

Pool Materials and Finishes

Choosing the right materials and finishes for your pool is essential for both its durability and visual appeal. Common pool materials include concrete, fiberglass, and vinyl, each with its own advantages and considerations.

Concrete pools offer flexibility in design and can be customized to suit your specific preferences. They are durable and can withstand various weather conditions. Fiberglass pools, on the other hand, come pre-fabricated and offer a smooth surface that is resistant to algae and stains. Vinyl pools are affordable and offer a wide range of design options, but they require regular liner replacement.

Consider the finishes of the pool's interior surface as well. From classic white plaster to more modern options like aggregate finishes or colorful tiles, the choice of finish will impact the pool's aesthetic appeal and maintenance requirements.

Collaborating with Pool Design Professionals

Working with pool design professionals, such as architects or landscape designers, is crucial during the planning and design phase. They have the expertise to transform your ideas into a practical and visually stunning pool design.

Collaborate closely with the design professionals, sharing your vision, budget, and preferences. They will provide valuable insights and recommendations based on their experience and knowledge of design principles. Together, you can create a pool design that meets your needs while considering factors such as safety, functionality, and local regulations.

Budgeting and Cost Considerations

As with any construction project, establishing a budget for your pool is essential. Consider not only the initial construction costs but also long-term maintenance expenses. It is recommended to obtain multiple quotes from reputable pool builders and factor in additional costs for landscaping, fencing, lighting, and water treatment systems.

Keep in mind that while there may be options to reduce costs, compromising on quality or essential features can lead to regrets in the long run. It is crucial to strike a balance between your budget and the desired pool design and features. Your pool design professionals can help you explore cost-saving options without sacrificing quality or functionality.

Pool Design Approval and Permits

Once your pool design is finalized, you will need to obtain the necessary approvals and permits before construction can begin. The requirements may vary depending on your location, so it is essential to familiarize yourself with local regulations and engage with the appropriate authorities.

Submit your pool design plans, including dimensions, features, and landscaping details, to the relevant authorities for review and approval. This process may take some time, so it is advisable to start early to avoid delays in your construction timeline.

By defining your pool's purpose, considering size and shape, choosing materials and finishes, collaborating with professionals, and establishing a budget, you will be well-prepared to move forward with the construction process. In the next chapter, we will explore the materials and equipment needed for swimming pool construction.

Chapter 3: Pool Construction Materials and Equipment

The selection of high-quality materials is crucial for the durability, functionality, and aesthetics of your pool.

There are various materials involved in pool construction, including structural materials, plumbing components, filtration systems, and surface finishes. Understanding the characteristics and options for each material will help you make informed decisions during the construction process.

Structural Materials

The structural integrity of your pool relies on the selection of robust and reliable materials.

The most common material used for the construction of swimming pools is reinforced concrete. Concrete pools offer strength, durability, and versatility in design. The pool shell is typically formed by pouring concrete into custom-built wooden or steel molds, known as formwork, and reinforcing it with steel bars or mesh.

In addition to concrete, other structural materials such as steel, aluminum, or composite materials may be used to reinforce specific areas of the pool, such as the walls or decking.

Plumbing Components

A properly functioning plumbing system is essential for maintaining the cleanliness and circulation of your pool water. The plumbing components include pipes, valves, fittings, and pumps that work together to ensure efficient water flow and filtration.

PVC (polyvinyl chloride) pipes are commonly used for pool plumbing due to their durability, resistance to corrosion, and ease of installation. Flexible PVC pipes are particularly useful for accommodating curved or irregular pool designs.

Valves and fittings, such as diverter valves, check valves, and union fittings, allow for control over water flow and facilitate maintenance and repairs.

Pool pumps are responsible for circulating water through the filtration system. They come in various sizes and types, including single-speed, dual-speed, and variable-speed pumps. Variable-speed pumps are more energy-efficient and provide greater control over water flow rates.

Filtration Systems

Proper filtration is essential for maintaining clear and healthy pool water. Filtration systems remove debris, contaminants, and microorganisms, ensuring that the water remains safe and inviting.

The two main types of pool filtration systems are sand filters and cartridge filters. Sand filters use a bed of fine sand to trap particles as water passes through, while cartridge filters utilize replaceable filter cartridges made of pleated fabric.

Additionally, some pools may incorporate additional filtration methods such as diatomaceous earth (DE) filters or advanced media filters for enhanced water clarity.

To ensure efficient filtration, it is important to properly size the filter system based on the pool's volume and anticipated usage.

Surface Finishes

The surface finish of your pool not only enhances its visual appeal but also affects its texture, durability, and maintenance requirements.

Plaster is a common choice for pool surfaces and can be finished in various colors. It offers a smooth and classic look but may require periodic re-plastering to maintain its appearance.

Aggregate finishes, such as pebble or quartz, consist of small stones mixed with plaster. They provide a textured surface that is more resistant to staining and can lend a natural aesthetic to the pool.

Tile finishes offer a luxurious and customizable option. Tiles are available in a wide range of colors, patterns, and materials such as ceramic, porcelain, or glass. They are durable and easy to clean but may require more maintenance compared to other finishes.

The choice of surface finish will depend on your aesthetic preferences, budget, and desired maintenance level.

Lighting and Electrical Systems

Proper lighting enhances the ambiance and safety of your pool area, allowing you to enjoy it even after the sun sets. Pool lighting options include underwater LED lights, fiber-optic lighting, or landscape lighting to illuminate the surrounding area.

Electrical systems are essential for powering pool equipment, such as pumps, lighting, and control systems. It is crucial to engage a qualified electrician to ensure compliance with electrical codes and safe installation practices.

In this chapter, we have explored the various materials and equipment required for swimming pool construction, including structural materials, plumbing components, filtration systems, surface finishes, lighting, and electrical systems. By selecting high-quality materials and understanding their functions, you can lay the foundation for a well-constructed and functional swimming pool. In the next chapter, we will discuss the pool construction process, from excavation to final touches

Chapter 4: Excavation and Foundation Preparation

Now, it's time to dive into the exciting phase of excavation and foundation preparation, where the physical transformation of your pool begins.

Excavation involves the removal of soil and earth to create a hole that will accommodate the pool structure. It is a crucial step that requires careful planning and execution to ensure proper alignment, dimensions, and structural integrity.

Site Preparation and Marking

Before excavation can commence, the pool construction team will survey and mark the pool's location on your property. This process involves using stakes, strings, and spray paint to outline the pool's shape, size, and desired orientation.

Site preparation is essential to clear the area of any obstacles such as trees, rocks, or existing structures that may interfere with the excavation process. It is crucial to consider any underground utility lines, such as electrical, water, or gas, to avoid any potential damage during excavation.

Excavation Process

Excavation can be performed using various methods, depending on the size and complexity of the pool design, as well as the soil conditions.

One common method is mechanical excavation, which involves using heavy machinery such as excavators or backhoes to remove soil and create the pool hole. The excavation team will carefully follow the marked guidelines to ensure the hole is excavated to the correct depth and dimensions.

In some cases, manual excavation may be necessary, especially for areas with limited access or sensitive surroundings. This process involves using hand tools and shovels to carefully remove the soil and create the pool hole.

During the excavation process, it is important to continually check the alignment and depth of the hole using laser levels or string lines to ensure accuracy. Any necessary adjustments should be made promptly to avoid complications later in the construction process.

Dealing with Soil and Drainage Challenges

The soil composition and drainage conditions at your construction site can significantly impact the excavation process and the stability of your pool. Different soil types, such as clay, sand, or loam, have varying properties that must be considered during excavation.

In areas with poor drainage or a high water table, additional measures may be necessary to prevent water accumulation around the pool. This can include the installation of drainage pipes or a sump pump system to divert excess water away from the pool area.

If the soil is unstable or prone to shifting, additional reinforcement measures, such as soil stabilization techniques or the use of geotextile fabrics, may be required to ensure the stability and longevity of the pool structure.

Foundation Preparation

Once the excavation is complete, the next step is to prepare the foundation of the pool. This involves leveling the excavated area, compacting the soil to provide a stable base, and addressing any potential issues that may affect the pool's structural integrity.

The pool construction team will carefully inspect the excavated hole, checking for any irregularities or soft spots. Any loose or unstable soil will be removed, and additional compaction may be performed to create a solid and level foundation.

In some cases, a layer of gravel or crushed stone may be added to enhance drainage and provide a stable base for the pool structure. This layer helps to prevent settling or shifting of the pool over time.

The excavation and foundation preparation phase is a critical step in swimming pool construction. Proper site preparation, accurate excavation, and the creation of a stable foundation are essential for the successful installation and longevity of your pool.

By working with experienced pool construction professionals and adhering to best practices, you can ensure that the excavation and foundation preparation process sets the stage for the next phases of pool construction. In the next chapter, we will explore pool plumbing and electrical systems, laying the groundwork for a fully functional pool

Chapter 5: Pool Plumbing and Electrical Systems

These systems play a crucial role in ensuring proper water circulation, filtration, and functionality of your pool.

Pool Plumbing System

The pool plumbing system consists of a network of pipes, valves, and fittings that work together to circulate water throughout the pool and its various components. It plays a vital role in maintaining water cleanliness and facilitating the operation of pool equipment.

The main components of a pool plumbing system include:

Skimmers: Skimmers are located at the waterline of the pool and are responsible for removing debris such as leaves, insects, and floating debris. They are equipped with baskets that trap larger debris before the water enters the filtration system.

Main Drains: Main drains are typically positioned at the bottom of the pool and aid in water circulation by allowing water to be drawn from the pool's floor. They help to evenly distribute chemicals and maintain consistent water temperatures throughout the pool.

Return Jets: Return jets are outlets located along the pool walls or floor. They distribute filtered and treated water back into the pool, creating circulation and maintaining water quality.

Plumbing Pipes: PVC (polyvinyl chloride) pipes are commonly used for pool plumbing due to their durability, corrosion resistance, and ease of installation. These pipes connect the various components of the pool plumbing system, allowing water to flow efficiently.

Valves and Fittings: Valves and fittings, such as gate valves, check valves, and union fittings, provide control over water flow and facilitate maintenance and repairs. They allow for adjustments in water circulation, such as controlling the flow between the skimmers and main drains or adjusting the water flow to different features like waterfalls or spa jets.

Proper installation and sizing of the plumbing system are crucial to ensure optimal water circulation, efficient filtration, and effective operation of pool equipment.

Pool Electrical System

The pool electrical system provides power to essential components such as pool pumps, lighting, heating systems, and control panels. It is important to work with a licensed electrician to ensure compliance with local electrical codes and safe installation practices.

The key components of a pool electrical system include:

Circuit Breakers and Panels: Circuit breakers protect electrical circuits from overloading and prevent electrical hazards. They are installed in electrical panels, which house the electrical connections and provide a centralized location for controlling the pool's electrical components.

Pool Pumps and Motors: Pool pumps are responsible for circulating water through the filtration system, while motors power various pool equipment such as water features or automatic pool cleaners. It is important to select energy-efficient pumps and motors to minimize electricity consumption and reduce operational costs.

Pool Lighting: Pool lighting not only enhances the aesthetics of your pool but also provides safety and ambiance. Underwater LED lights, fiber-optic lighting, or landscape lighting can be installed to illuminate the pool area during evening hours.

Control Systems: Pool control systems allow you to manage and automate various pool functions, such as adjusting water temperature, controlling lighting, and operating water features. These systems can be accessed remotely through mobile applications, providing convenience and flexibility.

Proper grounding, electrical insulation, and the use of waterproof and corrosion-resistant materials are essential in pool electrical system installation to ensure safety and longevity.

Safety Considerations

When dealing with pool plumbing and electrical systems, it is crucial to prioritize safety. Here are some important considerations:

Ground Fault Circuit Interrupter (GFCI): GFCIs are electrical safety devices that protect against electric shocks. They should be installed in all pool electrical circuits to provide additional protection.

Bonding and Grounding: Bonding and grounding systems are essential for electrical safety in and around the pool. They help to prevent electrical shock hazards by creating a path for electrical current to flow safely in the event of a fault.

Compliance with Electrical Codes: It is important to adhere to local electrical codes and regulations when installing pool electrical systems. This ensures that the installation meets safety standards and minimizes the risk of electrical hazards.

By paying attention to these safety considerations and working with experienced professionals, you can ensure the reliable and safe operation of your pool plumbing and electrical systems.

In the next chapter, we will discuss the installation of pool filters, pumps, and heaters, which are crucial for maintaining water clarity and temperature control in your swimming pool.

Chapter 6: Installing Pool Filters, Pumps, and Heaters

Pool filtration systems are responsible for removing debris, contaminants, and impurities from the water, ensuring a safe and enjoyable swimming experience.

Types of Pool Filters

There are different types of pool filters available, each with its own advantages and considerations. The three main types of pool filters are:

Sand Filters: Sand filters are the most common type of pool filters. They feature a tank filled with specially graded sand that traps debris and particles as water passes through. Sand filters are effective at removing larger particles and require periodic backwashing to flush out accumulated debris.

Cartridge Filters: Cartridge filters utilize replaceable filter cartridges made of pleated fabric. These filters provide a larger surface area for filtration, resulting in more efficient trapping of smaller particles. Cartridge filters necessitate less frequent upkeep in comparison to sand filters and can be effortlessly cleansed through rinsing or substituting the cartridges.

Diatomaceous Earth (DE) Filters: DE filters use a fine, powdered substance called diatomaceous earth, which coats the filter elements. DE filters offer the highest level of filtration, capable of capturing even the smallest particles. They require regular backwashing and replenishment of diatomaceous earth for optimal performance.

The choice of filter type will depend on factors such as the pool size, anticipated usage, and maintenance preferences. Consulting with a pool professional can help you determine the most suitable filter for your specific needs.

Pool Pumps

Pool pumps are the heart of the circulation system, responsible for moving water through the filtration system. They work in conjunction with the filter to ensure efficient water circulation and effective filtration.

When selecting a pool pump, consider the following factors:

Pump Size: The size of the pump should be appropriate for your pool's volume and specific hydraulic requirements. Oversized pumps can lead to excessive energy consumption, while undersized pumps may not provide sufficient water flow.

Pump Speed: Pool pumps are available in single-speed, dual-speed, and variable-speed models. Single-speed pumps operate at a constant speed, while dual-speed pumps offer the flexibility of running at high or low speeds. Variable-speed pumps allow for further customization of flow rates and are the most energy-efficient option.

Energy Efficiency: Opting for an energy-efficient pump can significantly reduce energy costs. Look for pumps with ENERGY STAR® certification or those that meet industry standards for energy efficiency.

Proper installation and regular maintenance of the pool pump are essential for optimal performance. This includes priming the pump, checking for any leaks, and ensuring the pump is adequately sized and aligned with the plumbing system.

Pool Heaters

Pool heaters allow you to extend the swimming season by maintaining a comfortable water temperature. They are particularly beneficial in regions with cooler climates or during colder months.

The two most common types of pool heaters are:

Gas Heaters: Gas heaters use natural gas or propane to heat the pool water. They are quick to heat the water and are suitable for both small and large pools. Gas heaters are popular for their ability to maintain consistent heat regardless of outdoor temperatures.

Heat Pumps: Heat pumps use electricity to transfer heat from the surrounding air to the pool water. They are more energy-efficient compared to gas heaters, making them a cost-effective option for heating pools. Heat pumps work best in regions with moderate climates.

When selecting a pool heater, consider factors such as your climate, desired water temperature, pool size, and budget. It is important to properly size the heater to ensure efficient operation and avoid excessive energy consumption.

In the next chapter, we will focus on pool decking and surrounding landscaping, where we will discuss various options for creating functional and aesthetically pleasing poolside areas.

Chapter 7: Pool Decking and Surrounding Landscaping

Now, let's shift our focus to the pool decking and surrounding landscaping, which play a significant role in enhancing the aesthetics and functionality of your pool area.

Choosing the Right Pool Decking Material

The pool deck is the area around the pool where you and your guests can relax, sunbathe, and enjoy outdoor activities. Selecting the right decking material is important as it should be durable, slip-resistant, and capable of withstanding constant exposure to water and sunlight.

Here are some popular options for pool decking:

Concrete: Concrete is a versatile and widely used material for pool decks. It offers durability, flexibility in design, and a range of finishes such as stamped, stained, or textured surfaces. Concrete can be customized to match various styles and provides a non-slip surface when properly treated.

Natural Stone: Natural stone, such as travertine, limestone, or slate, creates a luxurious and timeless look for pool decks. It offers natural beauty, durability, and slip resistance. However, natural stone can be more expensive and requires periodic sealing to maintain its appearance.

Pavers: Pavers are individual units made from materials like concrete, brick, or stone. They are available in a variety of shapes, sizes, and colors, allowing for endless design possibilities. Pavers offer excellent slip resistance, ease of installation, and the ability to replace individual units if needed.

Wood: Wood decking can provide a warm and natural aesthetic to your pool area. However, it requires regular maintenance, such as sealing, staining, and periodic refinishing, to protect it from water damage and decay. Choosing a durable, weather-resistant wood species, such as cedar or teak, is essential for longevity.

When selecting the pool decking material, consider factors such as budget, maintenance requirements, climate, and desired aesthetic appeal. Consulting with a professional can help you make an informed decision based on your specific needs.

Enhancing Poolside Landscaping

Landscaping around the pool area can create a visually appealing and inviting space. It helps to soften the pool's edges, provide privacy, and enhance the overall ambiance. Here are some key elements to consider when planning poolside landscaping:

Plants and Greenery: Choose plants that are well-suited to your climate, provide shade, and have a low shedding of leaves or flowers. Consider using a mix of trees, shrubs, and ornamental grasses to create a balanced and visually appealing landscape. Incorporating planters or flower beds near the pool deck can add color and fragrance to the area.

Hardscaping Elements: Integrate hardscaping elements such as retaining walls, pathways, or decorative stone features to add texture and visual interest. These elements can define different areas, provide seating options, and create a sense of cohesion with the pool deck.

Lighting: Outdoor lighting not only adds a touch of elegance but also enhances safety and functionality. Consider installing poolside lighting, pathway lights, and accent lights to create a warm and inviting atmosphere during evening hours.

Privacy Features: Depending on your preference and property layout, consider incorporating privacy features such as fencing, hedges, or strategic plantings to create a secluded and intimate pool area.

Safety Considerations

When designing pool decking and landscaping, it is crucial to prioritize safety. Here are some important safety considerations:

Slip Resistance: Choose decking materials and finishes that provide adequate slip resistance, especially when wet. Textured surfaces, non-slip coatings, or adding mats or rugs in high-traffic areas can help prevent slips and falls.

Drainage: Ensure proper drainage around the pool deck to prevent water accumulation and minimize the risk of slippery surfaces. Properly designed drainage systems can redirect water away from the pool area and prevent damage to the pool deck.

Safety Barriers: If required by local regulations, install safety barriers such as fences or gates around the pool area to prevent unauthorized access and ensure the safety of children and pets.

By considering these safety measures and design principles, you can create an attractive and functional pool area that complements your lifestyle and enhances your enjoyment of the space.

In the next chapter, we will discuss pool finishes and surface treatments, which contribute to the visual appeal and durability of your swimming pool

Chapter 8: Pool Finishes and Surface Treatments

Pool finishes not only enhance the overall appearance of your pool but also serve as a protective layer for the pool's structure. They provide a smooth and waterproof surface that is comfortable to touch and resistant to chemicals, UV rays, and the natural elements.

Common Pool Finish Options

There are several pool finish options available, each with its own unique characteristics and aesthetic appeal. Here are some of the most popular choices:

Plaster: Plaster is a traditional and widely used pool finish that consists of a mixture of white cement, aggregates, and water. It can be tinted to create different color options. Plaster offers a smooth and durable surface but may require periodic refinishing or resurfacing over time.

Pebble: Pebble finishes feature small, rounded pebbles mixed with plaster, creating a textured and visually appealing surface. Pebble finishes are known for their durability, resistance to staining, and ability to hide minor surface imperfections. They are available in a variety of colors and can give your pool a natural and organic look.

Tile: Tile finishes provide a luxurious and sophisticated appearance to the pool. Tiles come in various materials, such as ceramic, porcelain, or glass, and offer endless design possibilities. They are highly durable, resistant to chemicals and fading, and require minimal maintenance. Tile finishes can be applied to the entire pool or used as decorative accents and waterline borders.

Aggregate: Aggregate finishes combine small pebbles, glass beads, or quartz crystals with plaster to create a textured surface. They offer a unique and visually stunning appearance with a range of colors and textures to choose from. Aggregate finishes are known for their durability, resistance to stains and fading, and ability to create a non-slip surface.

Surface Treatments and Enhancements
In addition to pool finishes, there are various surface treatments and enhancements available to further enhance the aesthetics and functionality of your pool. Here are some popular options:

Waterline Tile: Installing tile along the waterline of the pool not only adds a decorative element but also helps to protect the pool's surface from stains caused by waterline deposits.

Mosaics: Mosaic designs can be incorporated into the pool finishes or used as decorative accents. These intricate patterns or images add a unique and personalized touch to your pool's visual appeal.

Color Enhancements: Some pool finishes allow for color enhancements, either through pigment additives or specialized coatings. These enhancements can create stunning visual effects, such as vibrant blue hues or shimmering finishes.

Non-Slip Coatings: To improve safety, especially in high-traffic areas or on pool decks, non-slip coatings can be applied to the pool's surface. These coatings provide increased traction and reduce the risk of slips and falls.

By carefully selecting the appropriate finish and considering additional surface treatments, you can create a pool that is visually stunning, comfortable to use, and built to withstand the test of time.

In the next chapter, we will delve into pool safety measures and regulations, ensuring that your pool is a secure and enjoyable space for everyone.

Chapter 9: Pool Safety Measures and Regulations

Safety should always be a top priority when it comes to owning a swimming pool. In this chapter, we will discuss important safety measures and regulations that are essential for ensuring the well-being of swimmers and preventing accidents or injuries.

Pool Safety Barriers

One of the key safety measures for any pool is the installation of proper barriers to restrict access to the pool area. Here are some common types of pool safety barriers:

Fencing: A pool fence acts as a physical barrier around the pool, preventing unsupervised entry. The fence should be at least four feet high and have self-closing and self-latching gates. The gate latch should be positioned out of the reach of children and should automatically latch when the gate closes.

Safety Covers: Safety covers are designed to cover the pool completely, creating a barrier that prevents accidental entry. These covers are typically made of strong, durable materials that can support the weight of a child or adult. Safety covers should be securely anchored to the pool deck and meet industry standards for strength and safety.

Alarms: Pool alarms can provide an additional layer of safety by alerting you when someone enters the pool area or when there is movement in the water. There are different types of alarms available, including gate alarms, door alarms, surface wave sensors, and underwater motion detectors. These alarms should be properly installed and regularly tested for optimal functionality.

Pool Safety Equipment

In addition to safety barriers, it is important to have the necessary safety equipment readily available near the pool area. Here are some essential pool safety equipment items:

Life Rings and Shepherd's Hooks: Life rings and shepherd's hooks are essential rescue tools that can be used to reach and assist a person in distress. They should be placed in a visible and easily accessible location near the pool.

First Aid Kit: A well-stocked first aid kit should be readily available in case of any injuries or emergencies. The kit should include basic supplies such as bandages, antiseptic solutions, scissors, gloves, and a CPR mask.

Safety Signage: Clear and visible safety signage should be posted in the pool area to provide important information and guidelines to swimmers. Signs can include rules for pool usage, depth markers, warnings about diving or running, and instructions for emergency procedures.

Pool Safety Regulations

It is crucial to be familiar with and comply with pool safety regulations and codes in your area. These regulations may include specific requirements for pool barriers, gate and latch mechanisms, alarms, and other safety measures. It is recommended to consult with local authorities or pool professionals to ensure that your pool meets all the necessary safety standards.

Educating Swimmers on Pool Safety

Proper education and awareness about pool safety are essential for preventing accidents and promoting responsible swimming practices. Ensure that all pool users, including family members, guests, and children, are educated on pool safety rules and guidelines. Teach swimmers about the importance of supervision, the dangers of swimming alone, and the appropriate use of pool equipment.

In the next chapter, we will explore water treatment and chemical balancing, which are crucial for maintaining clean and hygienic pool water.

Chapter 10: Water Treatment and Chemical Balancing

Maintaining clean and properly balanced water is essential for the health and enjoyment of your swimming pool. Let's see the importance of water treatment and chemical balancing to ensure crystal clear and hygienic pool water.

Water Testing

Regular water testing is a fundamental step in maintaining proper chemical balance in your pool. Testing allows you to monitor important parameters such as pH level, alkalinity, calcium hardness, and chlorine or sanitizer levels. You can use test kits or electronic testers specifically designed for pool water testing. Follow the instructions provided with the test kit to obtain accurate results.

pH Balance

The pH level of your pool water refers to its acidity or alkalinity. The ideal pH range for pool water is typically between 7.4 and 7.6. If the pH level is too low (acidic), it can cause skin and eye irritation, corrode pool equipment, and reduce the effectiveness of sanitizers. If the pH level is too high (alkaline), it can lead to cloudy water, scale formation, and reduced sanitizer efficiency.

To adjust the pH level:

If the pH is too low, add a pH increaser (such as sodium carbonate or soda ash) following the manufacturer's instructions.

If the pH is too high, add a pH reducer (such as sodium bisulfate or muriatic acid) following the manufacturer's instructions.

Always make gradual adjustments and retest the water after a few hours to ensure the desired pH range is maintained.

Alkalinity Balance

Total alkalinity refers to the ability of the pool water to resist changes in pH. The recommended alkalinity range is typically between 80 and 120 parts per million (ppm). Proper alkalinity helps stabilize the pH level and prevent rapid fluctuations.

To adjust alkalinity:

If the alkalinity is too low, add an alkalinity increaser (such as sodium bicarbonate) following the manufacturer's instructions.

If the alkalinity is too high, add an alkalinity reducer (such as muriatic acid) following the manufacturer's instructions.

It is important to note that adjusting alkalinity can also affect the pH level, so it's crucial to test and balance both parameters accordingly.

Sanitizer Levels

Sanitizers, such as chlorine or bromine, are essential for killing bacteria, viruses, and other microorganisms in pool water. The recommended sanitizer levels depend on the type of sanitizer used and may vary. It is important to maintain the proper sanitizer levels to ensure a safe and healthy swimming environment.

Regularly test the sanitizer levels and adjust accordingly by adding the appropriate amount of sanitizer product based on the test results. Follow the manufacturer's instructions and be mindful of any specific guidelines for the type of sanitizer you are using.

Calcium Hardness

Calcium hardness refers to the amount of dissolved calcium in the pool water. The recommended range for calcium hardness is generally from 200 to 400 ppm. Proper calcium hardness helps prevent corrosion, scale formation, and surface damage.

If the calcium hardness level is too low, you can increase it by adding a calcium hardness increaser product following the manufacturer's instructions. If the calcium hardness level is too high, dilution with fresh water may be necessary.

Regular Maintenance and Filtration

In addition to chemical balancing, regular maintenance and proper filtration are vital for keeping your pool water clean and clear. Follow these maintenance tips:

- Skim the pool surface to remove leaves, debris, and insects.
- Vacuum the pool to eliminate dirt and sediment.
- Backwash or clean the pool filter regularly to maintain its efficiency.
- Maintain proper water circulation by running the pool pump for an adequate duration each day.

Proper water treatment and chemical balancing are essential for maintaining clean, clear, and safe pool water.

In the next chapter, we will explore the basics of pool maintenance, including cleaning and vacuuming techniques, to keep your pool in pristine condition

Chapter 11: Pool Maintenance Basics

Regular maintenance is key to keeping your swimming pool clean, safe, and inviting. In this chapter, we will discuss the essential pool maintenance tasks that should be performed on a routine basis to ensure optimal pool conditions.

Skimming and Cleaning the Pool Surface
Skimming the pool surface is an important maintenance task that should be done daily or as needed. Use a pool skimmer net to remove leaves, debris, insects, and any other floating objects from the water surface. This prevents them from sinking to the bottom and clogging the pool's filtration system.

Additionally, make sure to regularly clean out the skimmer baskets to maintain proper water flow and prevent debris from obstructing the system.

Vacuuming the Pool

Vacuuming the pool helps remove dirt, sediment, and other particles that settle on the pool floor. There are different types of pool vacuums available, such as manual vacuums, automatic cleaners, or robotic cleaners. Follow these steps to vacuum your pool:

- Attach the vacuum head to the telescopic pole.
- Attach the vacuum hose to the vacuum head.
- Slowly lower the vacuum head and hose into the pool, ensuring that all air is expelled from the hose.
- Move the vacuum head across the pool floor, overlapping each stroke to cover the entire surface area.

- Pay extra attention to areas with visible dirt or debris.

Once you have vacuumed the entire pool, remove the vacuum equipment from the water and clean out any collected debris.

It is recommended to vacuum the pool at least once a week, or more frequently if needed.

Brushing the Pool Walls and Tile

Brushing the pool walls and tile helps remove algae, dirt, and other residues that can accumulate over time. Use a pool brush with nylon bristles or stainless steel bristles (for tiled areas) to gently scrub the walls, steps, and tile surfaces. Start from the top and work your way down, ensuring thorough coverage.

Focus on areas that are prone to algae growth or have visible stains. Regular brushing not only keeps your pool looking clean but also prevents the buildup of stubborn stains.

Cleaning the Pool Filter

The pool filter plays a crucial role in keeping the water clear and free of contaminants. Depending on the type of filter you have (sand, cartridge, or diatomaceous earth), it is important to follow the manufacturer's instructions for cleaning and maintenance.

For sand filters, backwashing is typically required when the pressure gauge indicates an increase in pressure. Backwashing involves reversing the flow of water through the filter to flush out trapped debris. After backwashing, don't forget to rinse the filter for a few minutes to ensure proper filtration.

Cartridge filters need periodic cleaning by removing the cartridges and rinsing them with a hose to remove accumulated debris. If the cartridges are heavily soiled, they may require soaking in a filter cleaner solution before rinsing.

Diatomaceous earth (DE) filters may require periodic cleaning by disassembling the filter and manually cleaning the filter grids or elements. Follow the manufacturer's instructions for proper cleaning techniques.

Regularly inspect the filter system, and if you notice any damage or issues, consult a professional for repairs or replacement.

Testing and Balancing Pool Chemistry
Regularly testing and balancing the pool water chemistry is crucial for maintaining safe and healthy swimming conditions. Refer to Chapter 10 for detailed information on water testing and chemical balancing.

Test the pool water regularly for pH, alkalinity, sanitizer levels, and calcium hardness. Based on the test results, adjust the chemical levels as needed using appropriate pool chemicals. This helps prevent issues such as algae growth, cloudy water, or skin and eye irritation.

Pool Cover Maintenance

If you have a pool cover, it is important to maintain it properly to extend its lifespan and ensure its effectiveness. Clean the cover regularly, removing any debris or leaves that may accumulate on its surface. Use a pool cover cleaner or mild detergent to remove dirt or stains. If your cover is solar or thermal, ensure it is properly positioned and secured to maximize its benefits.

Regular pool maintenance is essential for the longevity and enjoyment of your swimming pool. By incorporating skimming, vacuuming, brushing, filter cleaning, water testing, and cover maintenance into your routine, you can ensure a clean and well-maintained pool environment.

In the next chapter, we will discuss common pool issues and troubleshooting techniques to help you identify and resolve potential problems.

Chapter 12:
Troubleshooting
Common Pool Issues

As a pool owner, you may encounter various issues or problems that can affect the functionality and enjoyment of your pool. Let's now unravel some common pool issues and provide troubleshooting techniques to help you identify and resolve them effectively.

Cloudy or Discolored Water

Cloudy or discolored water is a common problem that can be caused by several factors, including improper water balance, insufficient filtration, or the presence of contaminants. Here are some steps to troubleshoot and address this issue:

Test the water: Check the pH, alkalinity, and sanitizer levels using a reliable test kit. Adjust the chemical balance as necessary to achieve the recommended ranges.

Increase filtration: Run the pool pump and filter for an extended period to enhance water circulation and filtration. Backwash or clean the filter if needed.

Shock the pool: If the water remains cloudy after balancing and increasing filtration, shock the pool by adding a higher dose of chlorine or non-chlorine shock treatment. Follow the product instructions and retest the water after a few hours.

Clarify the water: Use a pool clarifier or flocculant to help gather small particles together for easier removal through filtration or vacuuming.

Algae Growth

Algae can quickly multiply and cause green or slimy pool water. To troubleshoot and combat algae growth, follow these steps:

Test and balance the water: Ensure proper water balance by adjusting pH, alkalinity, and sanitizer levels. Algae growth is often favored by imbalanced water conditions.

Brush and vacuum: Brush the pool walls, steps, and surfaces to dislodge algae, and vacuum the pool thoroughly to remove any visible algae particles.

Shock treatment: Use a strong dose of chlorine or algaecide to kill existing algae. Follow the product instructions and maintain proper sanitizer levels afterward.

Algaecide maintenance: Regularly add a maintenance dose of algaecide to prevent future algae growth. Follow the product recommendations for dosage and frequency.

Low or Inadequate Water Circulation

Insufficient water circulation can lead to stagnant areas, poor filtration, and the accumulation of debris or contaminants. To troubleshoot this issue, consider the following steps:

Check the pump and filter: Inspect the pool pump and filter system for any clogs, obstructions, or mechanical issues. Clean or replace the filter media if necessary.

Verify the pump settings: Ensure that the pump is set to the correct speed or flow rate for optimal circulation. Consult the pump's manual or a pool professional if needed.

Adjust return jets: Ensure that the return jets are properly positioned to promote water movement and circulation. Aim them downward and at angles to create a gentle surface current.

Consider additional circulation aids: Install pool water features like waterfalls, fountains, or water jets to enhance water movement and circulation.

Persistent Green or Black Stains

Green or black stains on pool surfaces are often caused by algae or metal deposits. To troubleshoot and remove these stains, follow these steps:

Identify the stain type: Determine whether the stain is algae-based or caused by metals. You can do a simple test by placing a vitamin C tablet on the stain. If it lightens or disappears, it is likely a metal stain.

Treat algae stains: Follow the algae treatment steps mentioned earlier, including brushing, shock treatment, and algaecide use. Persistent stains may require additional targeted scrubbing or specialized stain removers.

Treat metal stains: If the stain is caused by metals, you can use a metal sequestrant or stain remover specifically designed for pools. Follow the product instructions carefully, as these products may require specific application methods.

Prevention: Maintain proper water balance and use a metal sequestrant regularly to prevent the recurrence of metal stains.

Equipment Malfunctions

Pool equipment, such as pumps, filters, heaters, or automation systems, may experience malfunctions over time. If you encounter equipment issues, consider the following troubleshooting steps:

Check power supply: Ensure that the equipment is receiving power by checking the circuit breaker, electrical connections, or switches.

Inspect for leaks: Examine the equipment and plumbing connections for any signs of leaks or damage. Tighten loose fittings or consult a professional for repairs.

Clean or replace filters: If the equipment is not functioning properly, clean or replace the filters to ensure proper flow and filtration.

Consult a professional: For complex equipment issues or if you're unsure about troubleshooting steps, seek the assistance of a pool professional or technician.

Regular maintenance, proper water balance, and prompt action can help ensure that your pool remains in optimal condition.

In the next chapter, we will explore pool repairs and renovations, providing guidance on addressing more extensive issues and improving the overall functionality and aesthetics of your pool.

Chapter 13: Pool Repairs and Renovations

Over time, swimming pools may require repairs or renovations to address structural issues, upgrade outdated features, or enhance the overall aesthetics. In this chapter, we will delve into the world of pool repairs and renovations, guiding you through the process of restoring and improving your pool.

Assessing Pool Damage

Before initiating any repairs or renovations, it is crucial to assess the extent of the pool damage. Common issues that may require attention include:

Cracks or leaks: Inspect the pool shell for any visible cracks or signs of water leakage. Pay attention to areas around fittings, skimmers, or tile lines.

Structural damage: Look for signs of shifting, sinking, or settling of the pool structure. These can manifest as uneven pool decks, bulging walls, or separation between the pool and surrounding features.

Plumbing or equipment issues: Check for leaks, clogs, or malfunctioning components in the pool plumbing and equipment system.

Surface deterioration: Assess the condition of the pool surface, such as worn-out plaster, fading paint, or damaged tiles.

Identifying and understanding the nature of the damage will help determine the appropriate repairs or renovations needed.

Pool Shell Repairs

For pool shell repairs, it is recommended to consult a professional pool contractor who specializes in structural repairs. Depending on the severity of the damage, the following repair methods may be employed:

Crack repair: Cracks in the pool shell can be repaired using epoxy injections, crack sealants, or specialized patching compounds. The pool contractor will assess the crack size and type to determine the most suitable repair approach.

Leak detection and repair: If there are signs of water leakage, the pool contractor will perform leak detection tests to pinpoint the source. Once identified, repairs can be made to fix the leaks, which may involve patching the affected area or replacing faulty plumbing components.

Structural reinforcement: In cases of severe structural damage, additional reinforcement may be necessary. This can include installing steel braces, rebar reinforcement, or even complete pool shell reconstruction. A professional pool contractor will assess the extent of the damage and recommend the appropriate structural reinforcement measures.

Upgrading Pool Features

Pool renovations often involve upgrading existing features to enhance functionality, energy efficiency, or visual appeal. Consider the following renovation options:

Pool equipment upgrades: Replace outdated pool pumps, filters, heaters, or automation systems with newer, more efficient models. This can improve energy consumption, reduce operating costs, and enhance overall performance.

Lighting enhancements: Install LED or fiber optic pool lights to create stunning visual effects and improve energy efficiency compared to traditional incandescent lights.

Water features: Add waterfalls, fountains, or bubblers to enhance the aesthetics and create a more enjoyable swimming experience.

Pool deck and coping: Upgrade the pool deck and coping materials to improve safety, durability, and aesthetics. Options include concrete, pavers, stone, or composite materials.

Surface refinishing: If the pool surface is worn or damaged, consider refinishing options such as plaster, pebble finishes, or tile replacements. This can rejuvenate the pool's appearance and extend its lifespan.

Consult with a professional pool contractor or designer to explore various renovation possibilities and select the best options for your specific needs and budget.

Pool Surround and Landscaping Enhancements

To complement your pool renovations, consider enhancing the pool surround and landscaping features:

Pool fencing: Upgrade or install a pool fence that adheres to local safety regulations. Choose from various materials such as wrought iron, aluminum, glass, or vinyl.

Poolside seating and lounging areas: Create comfortable seating and lounging spaces by adding patio furniture, outdoor sofas, or loungers. Incorporate shade structures like pergolas or umbrellas for sun protection.

Outdoor kitchens and dining areas: Construct an outdoor kitchen or dining area adjacent to the pool for convenient entertaining and alfresco dining experiences.

Landscaping and plantings: Use a combination of shrubs, flowers, trees, and decorative rocks to create a visually appealing and inviting poolside oasis. Consider low-maintenance plants that can withstand poolside conditions.

Engaging the services of a professional landscaper or landscape architect can help you design and implement the desired pool surround and landscaping enhancements.

Pool Renovation Permits and Regulations

Before embarking on any significant pool renovations, it is essential to research and comply with local building codes, permits, and regulations. Contact your local building department to inquire about any necessary permits, inspections, or specific requirements for pool repairs or renovations.

Pool repairs and renovations provide an opportunity to restore, upgrade, and transform your swimming pool into a rejuvenated and aesthetically pleasing space. Whether addressing structural issues, upgrading equipment, or enhancing the pool surroundings, professional guidance and careful planning will ensure successful pool renovations.

In the next chapter, we will discuss winterizing and seasonal pool care, providing guidance on how to protect your pool during the colder months and prepare it for the upcoming swimming season.

Chapter 14:
Winterizing and
Seasonal Pool Care

As the swimming season comes to an end, it's important to properly prepare your pool for the winter months and implement seasonal pool care practices. In this chapter, we will guide you through the process of winterizing your pool and provide tips for maintaining it during the offseason.

Pool Winterizing Preparation

Before winter arrives, it is essential to take the following steps to protect your pool from potential damage caused by freezing temperatures:

Clean the pool: Remove any debris, leaves, or dirt from the pool water using a skimmer net or pool vacuum. This will prevent the accumulation of organic matter during the offseason.

Balance the water chemistry: Test the water and adjust the pH, alkalinity, and sanitizer levels to the recommended ranges. Balanced water will help prevent scale buildup and corrosion.

Shock the pool: Before closing the pool, shock the water with a higher dose of chlorine to eliminate any remaining contaminants. Follow the product instructions and allow the water to circulate for several hours.

Remove and store accessories: Take out any pool accessories, such as ladders, handrails, or pool toys, and store them in a clean, dry place to prevent damage or deterioration.

Lower the water level: Lower the water level in the pool to below the skimmer and return jets. This prevents freezing and potential damage to the plumbing lines. Use caution and follow local guidelines regarding water level adjustments.

Pool Equipment Winterization
Properly winterizing your pool equipment will help protect it from freezing temperatures and extend its lifespan. Follow these steps to winterize the equipment:

Clean and backwash the filter: Thoroughly clean the pool filter and perform a backwash to remove any debris or contaminants. Allow the filter to dry completely before storing it.

Drain and winterize the plumbing: Drain all the water from the plumbing lines, including the pump, filter, heater, and any other equipment. Use compressed air to blow out any remaining water and prevent freezing. Consult a professional or refer to the equipment manuals for specific instructions.

Disconnect and store equipment: Disconnect the pump, filter, heater, and any other equipment from the power source. Clean and dry the equipment, then store it in a dry, protected area.

Secure the pool cover: Install a secure and properly fitting pool cover to keep debris out and provide an additional layer of protection during the winter months.

Seasonal Pool Care
Even during the offseason, it's important to perform regular maintenance tasks to keep your pool in good condition. Consider the following seasonal pool care practices:

Regular inspection: Periodically check the pool cover, ensuring it remains intact and free from damage. Remove any debris or standing water that may accumulate on the cover.

Snow removal: If you live in an area prone to heavy snowfall, periodically remove snow from the pool cover using a broom or a pool cover pump. Excessive snow can put pressure on the cover and potentially damage it.

Water level monitoring: Check the water level in the pool periodically to ensure it remains within the recommended range. Add water if necessary to maintain the proper level.

Algae prevention: Although the pool is not in use, continue to add a maintenance dose of algaecide to prevent algae growth. Follow the product instructions for dosage and frequency.

Regular maintenance: Inspect and maintain pool equipment throughout the offseason. Check for any leaks, damage, or signs of wear and address them promptly.

Seasonal Pool Care Supplies

To facilitate seasonal pool care, it's helpful to have the following supplies on hand:

Pool cover: Invest in a high-quality pool cover that fits securely and provides adequate protection against debris and harsh weather conditions.

Pool cover pump: A pool cover pump helps remove excess water from the cover and prevents damage.

Winterizing chemicals: Stock up on winterizing chemicals, including chlorine, algaecide, and stain preventers, to maintain water quality during the offseason.

Maintenance tools: Keep basic maintenance tools such as a skimmer net, pool brush, and pool vacuum for occasional cleaning and upkeep.

Properly winterizing your pool and implementing seasonal pool care practices will help protect your pool investment and ensure a smooth reopening when the swimming season returns. By following the guidelines provided in this chapter, you can confidently maintain your pool's condition and prolong its lifespan.

Conclusion

Throughout this comprehensive guide, we have covered various aspects of swimming pool construction and maintenance. Let's recap some of the key points discussed in the previous chapters:

Introduction to Swimming Pool Construction: We explored the different types of swimming pools, their benefits, and factors to consider when planning a pool construction project.

Planning and Designing Your Swimming Pool: This chapter highlighted the importance of proper planning, including site selection, pool design considerations, and obtaining necessary permits.

Pool Construction Materials and Equipment: We discussed the different materials and equipment used in pool construction, focusing on their features, durability, and maintenance requirements.

Excavation and Foundation Preparation: This chapter detailed the excavation process, soil evaluation, and proper foundation preparation to ensure a stable and structurally sound pool.

Pool Plumbing and Electrical Systems: We explored the installation of pool plumbing and electrical systems, emphasizing the significance of proper design, installation, and safety measures.

Installing Pool Filters, Pumps, and Heaters: This chapter covered the selection, installation, and maintenance of pool filtration, circulation, and heating systems to maintain water quality and temperature.

Pool Decking and Surrounding Landscaping: We discussed various pool decking options and landscaping ideas to enhance the aesthetics and functionality of the pool area.

Pool Finishes and Surface Treatments: This chapter focused on different pool surface finishes, including plaster, pebble, and tile, along with surface treatment techniques for longevity and visual appeal.

Pool Safety Measures and Regulations: We highlighted the importance of pool safety and adherence to local regulations, covering topics such as pool fencing, alarms, and safety covers.

Water Treatment and Chemical Balancing: This chapter provided guidelines for maintaining proper water chemistry, including testing, sanitization methods, and chemical balancing techniques.

Pool Maintenance Basics: We discussed the essential maintenance tasks, such as skimming, vacuuming, and brushing, to keep the pool clean and well-maintained.

Cleaning and Vacuuming the Pool: This chapter delved into more specific pool cleaning techniques, including manual and automatic vacuuming, and maintaining a clean pool environment.

Troubleshooting Common Pool Issues: We covered common pool problems, such as algae, cloudy water, and equipment malfunctions, along with troubleshooting tips and solutions.

Pool Repairs and Renovations: This chapter provided insights into pool repairs and renovations, including assessing damage, shell repairs, upgrading features, and enhancing the pool surroundings.

Winterizing and Seasonal Pool Care: The last chapter explained the importance of proper pool winterization and outlined seasonal pool care practices to protect the pool during the offseason.

Final Tips for Enjoying Your Pool

To conclude this guide, here are some additional tips to help you fully enjoy your swimming pool:

Regular Maintenance: Maintain a consistent pool maintenance schedule, including water testing, cleaning, and equipment inspections, to keep the pool in optimal condition.

Safety First: Always prioritize pool safety by following safety guidelines, ensuring proper supervision, and teaching swimming skills to family members and guests.

Professional Assistance: When in doubt or dealing with complex pool issues, seek the expertise of professional pool contractors or technicians for advice, repairs, or renovations.

Enjoyment and Relaxation: Remember that your pool is not just for swimming but also for relaxation and enjoyment. Create a poolside oasis with comfortable seating, lighting, and outdoor amenities.

Continuous Learning: Stay updated on the latest trends, technologies, and maintenance practices in the pool industry to enhance your pool ownership experience.

Final Thoughts

Swimming pool construction and maintenance require careful planning, attention to detail, and ongoing care. By following the guidelines presented in this guide, you can create a beautiful and well-maintained pool that provides endless hours of enjoyment for you, your family, and your friends.

Remember that each pool is unique, and individual circumstances may vary. Adapt the information provided in this guide to suit your specific needs and consult professionals as necessary. With proper construction, regular maintenance, and a commitment to safety, your swimming pool will continue to be a source of pleasure and relaxation for years to come.

We hope this guide has been informative and valuable to you. Dive in and enjoy your swimming pool adventure!